The
Case
for a
Creator

Participant's Guide

Resources by Lee Strobel

The Case for Christ

The Case for Christ audio

The Case for Christ — Student Edition (with Jane Vogel)

The Case for Christ curriculum (with Garry Poole)

The Case for Christmas

The Case for Christmas audio

The Case for a Creator

The Case for a Creator audio

The Case for a Creator — Student Edition (with Jane Vogel)

The Case for a Creator curriculum (with Garry Poole)

The Case for Easter

The Case for Faith

The Case for Faith audio

The Case for Faith — Student Edition (with Jane Vogel)

The Case for Faith curriculum (with Garry Poole)

The Case for the Real Jesus

The Case for the Real Jesus audio

Discussing the Da Vinci Code curriculum (with Garry Poole)

Discussing the Da Vinci Code discussion guide (with Garry Poole)

Exploring the Da Vinci Code (with Garry Poole)

Experiencing the Passion of Jesus (with Garry Poole)

Faith Under Fire curriculum series

God's Outrageous Claims

Inside the Mind of Unchurched Harry and Mary

Off My Case for Kids

Surviving a Spiritual Mismatch in Marriage (with Leslie Strobel)

Surviving a Spiritual Mismatch in Marriage audio

What Jesus Would Say

Other Resources by Garry Poole

The Complete Book of Questions

Seeker Small Groups

The Three Habits of Highly Contagious Christians

In the Tough Questions series:

Don't All Religions Lead to God?

How Could God Allow Suffering and Evil?

How Does Anyone Know God Exists?

Why Become a Christian?

Tough Questions Leader's Guide (with Judson Poling)

LEE STROBEL
AND GARRY POOLE

THE
CASE
FOR A
CREATOR

PARTICIPANT'S GUIDE

*A Six-Session Investigation of the
Scientific Evidence That Points toward God*

ZONDERVAN®

ZONDERVAN.com/
AUTHORTRACKER
follow your favorite authors

The Case for a Creator Participant's Guide
Copyright © 2008 by Lee Strobel and Garry Poole

Requests for information should be addressed to:
Zondervan, *Grand Rapids, Michigan 49530*

ISBN 978-0-310-28285-3

Interior design by Beth Shagene

Printed in the United States of America

08 09 10 11 12 13 14 • 20 19 18 17 16 15 14 13 12 11 10 9 8 7 6 5 4 3 2 1

CONTENTS

Special thanks to
Laura Allen and Jim Poole
for their outstanding writing and editing contributions.
Their creative insights and suggestions
took this guide to the next level.

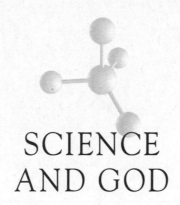

SCIENCE
AND GOD

I was convinced that science and faith were at odds — and that science definitely had the edge in the credibility department.... And rather than facing an "unyielding despair" that's implicit in a world without God, I reveled in my newly achieved freedom from God's moral strictures. For me, living without God meant living 100 percent for myself. Freed from someday being held accountable for my actions, I felt unleashed to pursue personal happiness and pleasure at all costs.... As a journalist, I was unshackled to compete without always having to abide by those pesky rules of ethics and morality. I would let nothing, and certainly nobody, stand between me and my ambitions.

Lee Strobel, *The Case for a Creator*

READ THIS!

If possible, read the following content in preparation for your group meeting. Otherwise, read it as follow-up.

The Case for a Creator, chapter 4: Where Science Meets Faith

Or, *The Case for a Creator Student Edition*, chapter 1: Science vs. God?

WATCH THIS!

DVD Introduction and Teaching Segment #1

For every DVD clip, space is provided to take notes on anything that stands out to you.

DISCUSS THIS!

1. How much confidence do you put in science as a source of truth? How did you develop the level of trust (or lack thereof) you currently have?

"Ironically, to say that science is the only begetter of truth is self-contradicting, because that statement in itself cannot be tested by scientific method. It's a self-defeating philosophical assumption."

Stephen C. Meyer

Think About This!

Some people claim that we live in a technological culture where science trumps all other forms of knowledge. Only science is rational; only science achieves truth. Everything else is mere belief and opinion. If something cannot be qualified or tested by the scientific method, then it cannot be true or rational. Science represents the empirical, the hard facts, and the experimentally proven. Everything else can be dismissed as being mere opinion, superstition — and mindless faith.

2. To what degree do you believe that only science is rational and everything else is mere opinion, superstition, or mindless faith?

"It was my science that drove me to the conclusion that the world was much more complicated than can be explained by science."

Cosmologist Allan Sandage

3. Has scientific progress made God unnecessary? Why or why not?

Think About This!

"The whole point of faith is to believe regardless of the evidence, which is the very antithesis of science."

Michael Shermer, publisher, *Skeptic* magazine

"Religion is something left over from the infancy of our intelligence; it will fade away as we adopt reason and science as our guidelines."

Atheistic philosopher Bertrand Russell

"Proof is only applicable to very rarefied areas of philosophy and mathematics.... For the most part we are driven to acting on good evidence, without the luxury of proof. There is good evidence of the link between cause and effect. There is good evidence that the sun will rise tomorrow. There is good reason to believe that I am the same man as I was ten years ago. There is good reason to believe my mother loves me and is not just fattening me up for the moment when she will pop arsenic into my tea. And there is good reason to believe in God. Very good reason. Not conclusive proof, but very good reason just the same.... I believe it is much harder to reject the existence of a supreme being than accept it."

Michael Green, *Faith for the Non-religious*

"You can't absolutely prove — or disprove — the existence of God."

Science philosopher Stephen C. Meyer

4. To what extent do you think it is possible to prove — or disprove — the existence of God? In terms of your own investigation, what level of evidence (or proof) would be sufficient for you to believe or disbelieve the existence of God? How likely is it that there would ever be enough evidence to eliminate your doubts (one way or the other)? What are the implications of your answers?

"For those who believe in God, no explanation is necessary. For those who do not, no explanation is possible."
Opening lines of the film
The Song of Bernadette

5. Do you agree with the assertion that if something cannot be quantified or tested, then it cannot be true or rational? Why or why not? What ways are there to confirm something exists without using the scientific method?

6. If science is, in fact, the search for truth, should scientists be free to consider the possibility of the supernatural if the evidence of cosmology, physics, and biochemistry points in that direction? Why or why not?

Optional Discussion Questions

- How much of the related chapter in *The Case for a Creator* were you able to read? What impacted you most? Which parts, if any, were most confusing to you?

- On a scale from 1 to 10, how opinionated do you think you are? Do you prefer to quickly settle into a specific perspective so you can bring matters to a close and move on, or do you tend toward suspending judgment for awhile so you can keep your options open?

- In general, how challenging is it for you to see or understand perspectives that differ from your own? If you were presented with hard evidence contrary to what you already strongly believe to be true, how open or reluctant would you be to change your position? How likely would you be to defend your initial position?

- Is there any limit to what man can discover scientifically? If so, what are the limits of science? If not, what are the possibilities?

- Which of the following statements do you think are true in spite of the fact that they cannot be tested or validated scientifically? What are some other examples of traits, values, or truths that exist but cannot be explained by science alone?

  - Humans have the capacity to love.

  - Humans have the capacity to self-reflect.

  - Humans have consciences.

  - Humans are creative creatures.

  - It is better to love than to hate.

  - It is wrong to murder an innocent person.

"I believe that the testimony of science supports theism. While there will always be points of tension or unresolved conflict, the major developments in science in the past five decades have been running in a strongly theistic direction. Science, done right, points toward God."

Stephen C. Meyer

WATCH THIS!

DVD Teaching Segment #2

DISCUSS THIS!

7. Describe an eureka moment you've experienced that illuminated or eliminated the necessity of God.

"The more deeply scientists see into the secrets of the universe, you'd expect, the more God would fade away from the hearts and minds."

Newsweek, July 20, 1998

8. Is it possible to believe in science and also believe in God? Can faith in God ever be rational? Why or why not?

"I didn't see any God out there."
Yuri Gagarin,
Soviet cosmonaut,
after orbiting Earth

Think About This!

"You will understand that my atheism was inevitably based on what I believed to be the finding of the sciences, and those findings, not being a scientist, I had to take on trust."

C. S. Lewis, *Surprised by Joy*

"I'd have to say that the biggest reason why I don't believe in god is because there is no proof of his existence. Throughout the millions of years that man has been on earth, there has never been any solid evidence that there is a creator. If there is a god, wouldn't he want as many followers as possible? Why leave any doubt? Why not come to earth and tell everyone he exists? Or, better yet, make it so that everyone knows he is there."

Norm, in an online discussion

9. Which of the following "isms" most accurately reflects your current position? What influences or factors prompted you to arrive at this perspective? How long have you held this position?

- **Atheism:** the disbelief in the existence of God
- **Deism:** the belief in a supreme being who remains unknowable and untouchable and permits the universe to run itself according to natural laws
- **Theism:** belief in the existence of God
- **Pantheism:** the belief that God and the universe are one
- **Polytheism:** the belief in many gods
- **Agnosticism:** the belief that knowledge of the existence or nonexistence of God is impossible
- **Fideism:** the belief that matters of religion are not supported by evidence or reason and all that is required is faith

"All I have seen teaches me to trust the Creator for all I have not seen."
Ralph Waldo Emerson

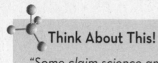

Think About This!

"Some claim science and faith are fundamentally at odds. Others have said science and faith represent two separate and distinct realms that don't and can't interact with each other. However, I personally take a third approach, which is that scientific evidence actually supports theistic belief. In fact, across a wide range of sciences, evidence has come to light in the last fifty years which, taken together, provides a robust case for theism. Only theism can provide an intellectually satisfying causal explanation for all of this evidence."

Stephen C. Meyer

10. Are science and faith at odds? Can science and faith *ever* be compatible? Must a science-minded person reject religious beliefs? Explain your answers.

"God gave us ... two powerful and well-matched abilities: to prove things we find hard to believe and to believe in things we find hard to prove."
Michael Guillen, *Can a Smart Person Believe in God?*

Think About This!

"I believe only and alone in the service of Jesus Christ. In him is all refuge and solace."

Johannes Kepler, who discovered the laws
of planetary motion and elliptical orbits

"At the center of every human being is a God-shaped vacuum which can only be filled by Jesus Christ."

Blaise Pascal, father of the mathematical theory
of probability and combinational analysis

"If we need an atheist for a debate, I'd go to the philosophy department — the physics department isn't much use."

Charles Coulson, an architect of Molecular Orbital Theory

"I think of God as the greatest scientist. We human scientists have an opportunity to understand the elegance and wisdom of God's creation in a way that is truly exhilarating. When a scientist discovers something that no human knew before, but God did — that is both an occasion for scientific excitement and, for a believer, also an occasion for worship."

Francis Collins, director of the Human Genome Project,
which first mapped human DNA

11. Do you think someone can be an unbiased scientist and religious at the same time? For example, can a Christian draw scientific conclusions in an unbiased way? What about an atheist?

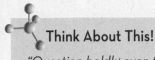

Think About This!

"Question boldly even the existence of God."

Thomas Jefferson

"Do not be afraid to be free thinkers. If you think strongly enough, you will be forced by science to the belief in God."

William Thompson, physical scientist and teacher

"Let's have a new period in the history of science where we have methodological rules that actually foster the unfettered seeking of truth. Scientists should be allowed to follow the evidence wherever it leads — even if it leads to a conclusion that makes some people uncomfortable."

Stephen C. Meyer

12. To what extent can we separate ourselves from our own biases? How much do our religious or atheistic preconceived notions and worldview taint the conclusions we draw? How might *your* current view of God—positive or negative—affect the way you assess the scientific evidence for his existence?

"Science and faith are not at war. When scientific evidence and biblical teaching are correctly interpreted, they can and do support each other. I'd say to anyone who doubts that: investigate the evidence yourself."

Stephen C. Meyer

Optional Discussion Questions

• With so many compelling and contradictory ideas out there, how does anyone know what to believe? What determining factors influence what you *do* believe? How sure are you about what you think you know for certain?

• Generally speaking, what percentage of scientific claims is indeed accurate? What percentage of what you were taught in school about science do you think is still considered valid today?

• What's the difference, if any, between a scientific theory and a scientific fact?

• Because scientific theories can change over time, how reliable is what we learn from science today? To what extent do you think future scientific discoveries will disprove current scientific understanding?

• Do most people you know believe that Christianity and evolution are either/or concepts or both/and ideas? Do you agree with Lee's conclusion that if life emerged out of naturalistic circumstances, God is out of a job?

• When Orville and Wilbur Wright persisted in experimenting with their flying machines (despite contrary opinion), to what extent did they test the limits of both science and faith? Were they driven more by science or by faith?

• Physicist John Polkinghorne asserts that science and religion are friends, not foes, united by the common quest for knowledge. Do you agree with this assertion? Are you open to the possibility? Why or why not?

• It has been said that scientists are not mere objective thinking machines but are driven by philosophical and emotional factors as well. To what degree do you think the motive of a scientist affects the validity of his or her theories? In other words, are the motivations behind a scientific theory independent of its scientific worth or are scientific conclusions in some ways really self-fulfilling prophecies?

WATCH THIS!

DVD Wrap-up/Lee's Perspective

In which direction — toward a Creator, or away from one — do you think the current arrow of science is pointing? What piece of evidence is most influencing your answer at this point?

"Many scientists are now driven to faith by their very work."
Allan Sandage

BETWEEN SESSIONS

Personal Reflection

"For I know the plans I have for you," declares the LORD, "plans to prosper you and not to harm you, plans to give you hope and a future. Then you will call upon me and come and pray to me, and I will listen to you. You will seek me and find me when you seek me with all your heart."

Jeremiah 29:11–13 NIV

• Do you gravitate toward or away from scientific inquiry? What about religious inquiry? How curious are you about God?

• Carefully meditate on the above verses from Jeremiah and just imagine these are God's words to you personally. What is your response? Are you skeptical? Bemused? Cynical? Or do you feel a spark of hope that this concept might be real? Try this exercise: Suspend your disbelief, just for a moment, and consider the possibility that God is real, that he cares about you and invites you to seek and find him. How does this possibility impact you?

• Now reread the promise made to you in the last sentence of the Jeremiah passage. What if God is real and keeps all his promises? Notice, though, that the promise is conditional—you must do your part. How willing are you to sincerely seek truth with your whole heart and to follow the evidence wherever it leads? What might hold you back from such an open-minded search?

• Jesus once had a conversation with one of his followers who admitted to him, "Lord, I believe, now help me with my unbelief!" Can you relate in any way to this man's honest and heartfelt plea? How surprising is it to you to discover that the Bible identifies many people who faced doubts about God, and yet he answered them? You can rest assured that God welcomes your objections, questions, and doubts—and that he even invites you to come to him with your unbelief!

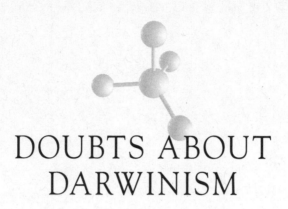

DOUBTS ABOUT DARWINISM

It was no accident that my admiration for scientific thinking was developing at the same time that my confidence in God was waning. In Sunday school and confirmation classes during my junior high school years, my "why" questions weren't always welcomed. So the seeds of my atheism were sown as a youngster when religious authorities seemed unwilling or unable to help me get answers to my questions about God. My disbelief flowered after discovering that Darwinism displaces the need for a deity. And my atheism came to full bloom when I studied Jesus in college and was told that no science-minded person could possibly believe what the New Testament says about him.

Lee Strobel, *The Case for a Creator*

READ THIS!

If possible, read the following content in preparation for your group meeting. Otherwise, read it as follow-up.

The Case for a Creator, chapter 2: The Images of Evolution

The Case for a Creator, chapter 3: Doubts about Darwinism

Or, *The Case for a Creator Student Edition*, chapter 3: Exploring Evolution

WATCH THIS!

DVD Teaching Segment #1

For every DVD clip, space is provided to take notes on anything that stands out to you.

DISCUSS THIS!

1. What's your immediate reaction to the illustration above? What thoughts or emotions does this picture elicit in you?

2. Describe Darwinian evolution as you currently understand it. Is it a theory or a fact? How has Darwinism evolved over time? What do you think people usually mean by the term "evolution"? What about the phrase "natural selection"?

"If you go back far enough, we and the chimps share a common ancestor. My father's father's father's father, going back maybe a half-million generations — about five million years ago — was an ape."
Walter Cronkite

3. Can you recall when you first were exposed to Darwin's theory of evolution? What was the setting? What was your reaction at the time? In what ways have your attitudes toward Darwinism evolved since then?

4. If you are familiar with the Stanley Miller experiment that Lee Strobel discussed in the DVD clip, describe the setting in which you first became aware of it. To what extent did the original results of this experiment influence you as they did Lee?

The Stanley Miller Experiment

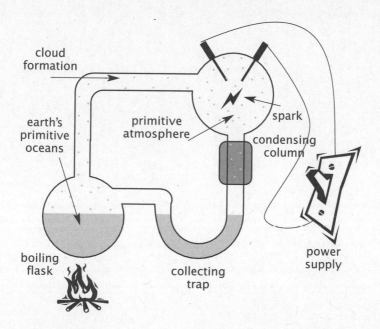

cloud formation

earth's primitive oceans

primitive atmosphere

spark

condensing column

boiling flask

collecting trap

power supply

The Old Story of Science

Miller used the hydrogen-rich mixture of methane, ammonia, and water vapor to demonstrate how the early atmosphere created amino acids, the building blocks of life.

The New Story of Science

Scientists today know that these were not the elements of the primitive atmosphere on earth. Miller's experiment has been repeated many times using the correct atmospheric components: carbon dioxide, nitrogen, water vapor, and very little hydrogen. The results are always the same: this mixture produces at best formaldehyde, but not amino acids, the building blocks of life.

5. Summarize the initial conclusion ("the old story of science") behind the Miller experiment. Does this conclusion make sense to you? Why or why not? What questions does it raise for you?

"The march of science has clearly left Miller's experiment in the dust, even if some textbooks haven't yet noticed."

Lee Strobel

6. Recap the results that have since discredited the initial conclusion drawn from the Stanley Miller experiment ("the new story of science").

Think About This!

"Even if scientists could somehow manage to produce amino acids from the correct mixture of elements of the early atmosphere, how far would they be from creating a living cell? You would have to get the right number of the right kinds of amino acids to link up to create a protein molecule — and that would still be a long way from a living cell. Then you'd need dozens of protein molecules, again in the right sequence, to create a living cell. The odds against this are astonishing. The gap between nonliving chemicals and even the most primitive living organisms is absolutely tremendous. The problem of assembling the right parts in the right way at the right time and at the right place, while keeping out the wrong material, is simply insurmountable."

Biologist Jonathan Wells

7. Read the "Think About This!" quote above regarding the low probability of amino acids ever producing life. Do you agree or disagree with this reasoning? Explain your answer.

"If you meet somebody who claims not to believe in evolution, that person is ignorant, stupid, or insane, (or wicked, but I'd rather not consider that)."
Atheist and evolutionary biologist Richard Dawkins

Optional Discussion Questions

- How much of the related chapters in *The Case for a Creator* were you able to read? What impacted you most?

Ernst Haeckel's Drawings of Embryos

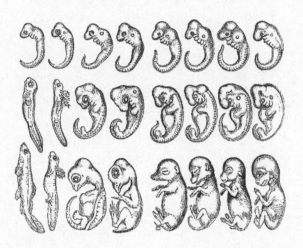

The Old Story of Science	*The New Story of Science*
A nineteenth-century German biologist, Ernst Haeckel, drew sketches to support Darwin's assertion that the striking similarities in the early stages of embryos of various animals indicate that all organisms share a common ancestor.	The so-called similarities of early embryos are not accurate when actual photos of embryos are compared to the sketches. The drawings misrepresent the embryos. Furthermore, Haeckel cherry-picked his examples by choosing representatives closest to his predetermined idea. Finally, Haeckel's sketches represent the midpoint of embryonic development rather than the early stages.

- If you can, describe the setting in which you first became familiar with Haeckel's drawings. Explain the point of Haeckel's drawings and his original theory behind them. Does this theory make sense to you? Why or why not? What questions does it raise for you?

- How does the fact that Haeckel's drawings were found to be inaccurate affect your opinion of the theory that all species evolved from one common ancestor? What is your response to the opinion held by some that although the Haeckel sketches are inaccurate, they still teach a concept that's basically true? Explain.

• It has been suggested that Haeckel had predetermined ideas that shaped his conclusions. Do you suspect that this may in fact be the case? Why or why not?

• University of Chicago biology philosopher Paul Nelson wrote, "The problem with Haeckel's drawings wasn't just that they were inaccurate, they were actually false in many cases. But the real damage was done when these drawings entered into biology textbooks decades ago and they've never really been taken out.... It's really damaged our understanding of development and our understanding of biology in general." Why do you think Haeckel's drawings, misleading as they were, continued to be published in textbooks?

• To what extent do you trust what your schools taught about evolution?

• Stephen C. Meyer among others believes it's contradictory to say that God guides an inherently unguided natural process or that God designed a natural mechanism as a substitute for his design. Do you think it is possible to believe in Darwinian evolution and still believe in the existence of God, or are evolution and creationism mutually exclusive? Explain your answer.

• Which of the following quotes do you agree with most? Least? Why?

> "I think people who believe that life emerged naturalistically need to have a great deal more faith than people who reasonably infer that there's an Intelligent Designer."
>
> Walter Bradley, *The Mystery of Life's Origin*

> "The more you understand the significance of evolution, the more you are pushed away from an agnostic position and towards atheism."
>
> Oxford evolutionist Richard Dawkins

> "As for me, I finally came to the point where I realized that I just didn't have enough faith to maintain my belief in Darwinism. The evidence in my estimation was simply unable to support its grandest and most sweeping claims."
>
> Lee Strobel

WATCH THIS!

DVD Teaching Segment #2

"No educated person any longer questions the validity of the so-called theory of evolution, which we now know to be a simple fact."
Evolutionary biologist Ernst Mayr

DISCUSS THIS!

8. If you can, describe the setting in which you first became familiar with the diagram called Darwin's "tree of life." What's the theory behind Darwin's tree of life? Does it make sense to you? Why or why not? What questions does it raise for you?

Darwin's "Tree of Life"

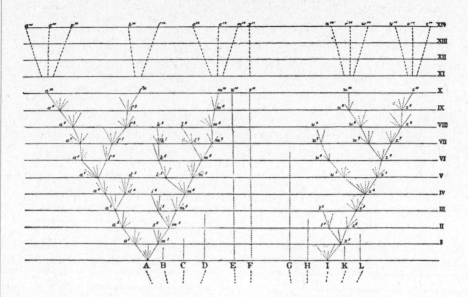

The Old Story of Science

All living creatures have a common ancestor. Starting with an ancient ancestor at the bottom, the tree blossoms upward into limbs, branches, and twigs that represent life evolving with increasing diversity and complexity. If a population were exposed to one set of conditions, and another part of the population experienced other conditions, then natural selection would modify the two populations in different ways. Over time, one species could produce several varieties, and if these varieties continued to diverge, they would eventually, over an enormous amount of time, become separate species. This theory predicts a long history of gradual divergence from a common ancestor, with differences slowly becoming bigger and bigger until we get the major differences we have now.

The New Story of Science

The fossil evidence to this day shows the opposite effect: a rapid appearance of phylum-level differences in what's called the Cambrian explosion. There is evidence of micro-evolution (changes within a species), but there are no conclusive examples of macro-evolution (transitional forms between major kinds of creatures). In short, the Cambrian explosion has uprooted Darwin's tree.

Fast Fact

Micro-evolution: *Comparatively minor, gradual evolutionary change involving the accumulation of variations within a species*

Macro-evolution: *Gradual evolution that results in relatively large and complex changes (as in species formation)*

9. According to the "Fast Fact" definitions above, what is the main difference between micro-evolution and macro-evolution? Give examples of the evidence that might support one or both forms of the evolutionary process. Which type do you see more evidence for in the world around you? In your estimation, which type of evolution is best represented by Darwin's tree of life? Elaborate.

"If you consider all the evidence, Darwin's tree is false as a description of the history of life. It's not even a good hypothesis at this point."

Jonathan Wells

Think About This!

"The most obvious and gravest objection which can be urged against my theory [is the fossil record]. Why, if species have descended from other species by insensibly fine gradations, do we not everywhere see innumerable transitional forms?"

Charles Darwin, *The Origin of Species*

10. What do you think Darwin would say today about the fact that the fossil record has never supported his theory of a gradual evolutionary process?

Fast Fact

The Cambrian was a geographical period that scientists believe began a little more than 540 million years ago. The Cambrian explosion has been called the "Biological Big Bang" because the exquisitely preserved Cambrian fossils reveal that the body plans for virtually every major animal phyla appeared, not gradually and slowly as Darwin had speculated, but, instead, with astonishing suddenness.

11. If all living organisms descended from the same primitive life form, as Darwin's tree of life suggests, does it follow that the rock strata of the earth would be filled with the transitional fossils needed to complete this great evolutionary chain? What do you think accounts for the inability to unearth such fossils up to this point in time?

 Think About This!

"Who knows how natural history might be rewritten next week by a discovery that will be made in a fossil dig somewhere? Is it possible that someone will discover a fossil bed somewhere that will suddenly fill in the gaps? Not likely. It hasn't happened after all this time, and millions of fossils have already been dug up. There are certainly enough good sedimentary rocks from before the Cambrian era to have preserved ancestors if there were any. The Cambrian explosion is too big to be masked by flaws in the fossil record."

Jonathan Wells

"The universal experience of paleontology is that while the rocks have continually yielded new and exciting and even bizarre forms of life ... what they have never yielded is any of Darwin's myriads of transitional forms. Despite the tremendous increase in geological activity in every corner of the globe and despite the discovery of many strange and hitherto unknown forms, the infinitude of connecting links has still not been discovered and the fossil record is about as discontinuous as it was when Darwin was writing Origin. The intermediates have remained as elusive as ever and their absence remains, a century later, one of the most striking characteristics of the fossil record."

Molecular geneticist Michael Denton,
Evolution: A Theory in Crisis

12. Read the following quote from Jonathan Wells:

> I believe science is strongly pointing toward design. To me, as a scientist, the development of an embryo cries out, "Design!" The Cambrian explosion — the sudden appearance of complex life, with no evidence of ancestors — is more consistent with design than evolution.... The origin of life certainly cries out for a designer. None of these things make as much sense from a Darwinian perspective as they do from a design perspective. When you analyze all the most current affirmative evidence from cosmology, physics, astronomy, biology, and so forth — well, I think you'll discover that the positive case for an intelligent designer becomes absolutely compelling.
>
> My conclusion is that the case for Darwinian evolution is bankrupt. The evidence for Darwinism is not only grossly inadequate, it's systematically distorted. I'm convinced that sometime in the not-too-distant future — I don't know, maybe twenty or thirty years from now — people will look back in amazement and say, "How could anyone have believed this?" Darwinism is merely materialistic philosophy masquerading as science, and people are recognizing it for what it is.

To what extent do you agree with Wells' assessment? In what ways do you disagree? In your opinion, what would need to happen before most people would reach his final conclusion? How likely do you think it is that people would someday say, "How could anyone have believed this?" Explain.

13. On a scale from 1–10, how strongly do you believe Darwin's theory of evolution is accurate? To what extent has it been proven? Has the evidence presented in this session in any way affected your opinion of evolution? If so, how? If not, why not?

Fast Fact

Intelligent Design Theory, ascribed to by a growing number of scientists, holds that certain features of the universe and of living things are best explained by an Intelligent Cause, not an undirected process such as natural selection.

Think About This!

"We are skeptical of claims for the ability of random mutation and natural selection to account for the complexity of life.... Careful examination of the evidence for Darwinian theory should be encouraged."

A Scientific Dissent from Darwinism,
signed by more than 600 scientists with
doctorates from a variety of institutions

"The claim that all skeptics about Darwinian orthodoxy are Christian fundamentalists stands refuted by me. I am neither a Christian nor a fundamentalist, but lots and lots of people are skeptical in the scientific community."

David Berlinski, PhD, Princeton University

"Scientists who utterly reject evolution may be one of our fastest-growing controversial minorities.... Many of the scientists supporting this position hold impressive credentials in science."

Larry Hatfield in Science Digest

"There is no encompassing theory of human evolution. Alas, there never really has been."

Anthropologist F. Clark Howell

"The controversy in modern times is not between science and religion, it's between two different interpretations of the same scientific evidence. It's not science vs. religion, it's science vs. science."

Stephen C. Meyer, PhD, History and Philosophy
of Science, Cambridge University

Optional Discussion Questions

The Archaeopteryx Missing Link

The Old Story of Science

Darwin suggested that the fossil record was incomplete and predicted that future archeological findings would vindicate him by demonstrating the missing links of innumerable transitional forms. Two years later, in 1861, scientists unearthed the archaeopteryx in a German quarry. A creature with the wings, feathers, and a wishbone of a bird but with a lizard-like tail and claws on its wings, it was hailed as the missing link between reptiles and birds.

The New Story of Science

"The archaeopteryx is not an ancestor of any modern birds; instead it's a member of a totally extinct group of birds."

Paleontologist Larry Martin,
University of Kansas

"It's a bird with modern feathers, and birds are very different from reptiles in many important ways — their breeding system, their bone structure, their lungs, their distribution of weight and muscles. It's a bird, that's clear — not part bird and part reptile."

Biologist Jonathan Wells

- If you can, describe the setting in which you first became familiar with the *archaeopteryx*. Describe the explanation behind the *archaeopteryx* missing link. Does it make sense to you? Why or why not? What questions does it raise for you?

- Speculate on some of the possible explanations for the zeal surrounding the scientifically incorrect conclusions regarding the alleged "transitional" fossils. In your opinion, why do scientists cling to outdated information related to evolution?

- If you were a juror and the following four "exhibits" were presented to you as evidence for the truth of Darwinism, would you say you have proof beyond any reasonable doubt? Why or why not?

  - The Stanley Miller experiment
  - Ernst Haeckel's drawings of embryos
  - Darwin's "tree of life"
  - The *archaeopteryx* missing link

WATCH THIS!

DVD Wrap-up/Lee's Perspective

In which direction—toward a Creator, or away from one—do you think the current arrow of science is pointing? What piece of evidence is most influencing your answer at this point?

BETWEEN SESSIONS

Personal Reflection

And God said, "Let the water teem with living creatures, and let birds fly above the earth across the vault of the sky." So God created the great creatures of the sea and every living and moving thing with which the water teems, according to their kinds, and every winged bird according to its kind. And God saw that it was good. God blessed them and said, "Be fruitful and increase in number and fill the water in the seas, and let the birds increase on the earth." ... And God said, "Let the land produce living creatures according to their kinds: livestock, creatures that move along the ground, and wild animals, each according to its kind." And it was so. God made the wild animals according to their kinds, the livestock according to their kinds, and all the creatures that move along the ground according to their kinds. And God saw that it was good.

Genesis 1:20 – 22, 24 – 25

- Growing up, how did what you learned about evolution affect your spiritual outlook or influence your beliefs about God? To what degree do you consider yourself to be open-minded regarding the issue of evolution? How willing are you to be challenged by new discoveries that may differ from what you've learned in the past?

- Think about an occasion when you had a significant understanding or belief exposed as inaccurate. How long had you held your erroneous view before it was somehow corrected? How did the process of "discovery" make you feel at the time? Resistant, embarrassed, angry? Or, as a truth-seeker, were you grateful to find out the truth of the matter?

- To what extent do you feel that doubts you may have had regarding God's existence were unacceptable and unwelcome? What were the circumstances or situations that fostered such attitudes in others around you? How might those past experiences impact the intensity of your spiritual search now?

• According to Genesis 1:20–22, 24–25, what exactly does the Bible claim to be true about the origin of the species? What does it say about each species' offspring? Do the creatures appear suddenly, as the Cambrian explosion and the fossil record seem to indicate, or do they form gradually over time, as Darwinian macro-evolutionists hold? Which scientific evidence or theory aligns most closely with what the Bible teaches?

• The Bible describes the Creator as a "God of knowledge" and says that his wisdom far surpasses that of any mere human. Are you surprised to learn that this same God promises to give wisdom to anyone who genuinely asks for it, including *you*? Why not go to God now in prayer and ask for wisdom regarding the origin—and perhaps even the meaning—of life?

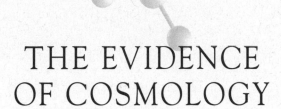

THE EVIDENCE OF COSMOLOGY

My eyes scanned the magazines at the newsstand near my home. A beautiful woman graced Glamour. Sleek, high-performance cars streaked across the front of Motor Trend. And there on the cover of Discover magazine, sitting by itself, unadorned, floating in a sea of pure white background, was a simple red sphere. It was smaller than a tennis ball, tinier than a Titleist—just three quarters of an inch in diameter, not too much bigger than a marble. As staggering as it seemed, it represented the actual size of the entire universe when it was just an infinitesimal fraction of one second old. The headline cried out: Where Did Everything Come From?

Lee Strobel, *The Case for a Creator*

READ THIS!

If possible, read the following content in preparation for your group meeting. Otherwise, read it as follow-up.

The Case for a Creator, chapter 5: The Evidence of Cosmology

Or, *The Case for a Creator Student Edition,* chapter 2: Beginning with a Bang

WATCH THIS!

DVD Teaching Segment #1

For every DVD clip, space is provided to take notes on anything that stands out to you.

---

*"The universe is all there is,
or ever was, or ever will be."*

Astronomer Carl Sagan

DISCUSS THIS!

1. Why do you think the issue about how the universe began is controversial for many people?

Fast Fact

Cosmologist: *A scientist who studies the origin of the universe*

2. Do you believe the universe has always existed in an eternal unchanging state? Or do you think the universe had an absolute beginning somewhere in the finite past? Give reasons for your opinion. Which position were you taught growing up?

"It seems impossible that you could get something from nothing, but the fact that once there was nothing and now there is a universe is evident proof that you can."
Bill Bryson, *A Short History of Nearly Everything*

3. The assumption ever since the ancient Greeks has been that the material world is eternal. Christians have denied this on the basis of biblical revelation, but secular science always assumed the universe's eternality. What do you think was the rationale behind why scientists once believed the universe always existed?

4. Read the following excerpt from the DVD clip:

> In 1929, theoretical predictions were confirmed with empirical data. At the Mount Wilson Observatory overlooking Los Angeles, astronomer Edwin Hubble studied light from distant galaxies. Hubble determined that galaxies beyond our Milky Way were moving away from us at a speed proportional to their distance from the earth. The more distant the galaxy, the faster it is receding. Hubble's landmark discovery led most astronomers and physicists — including Albert Einstein — to a similar conclusion: if the universe is continually expanding, then at earlier points in its history, it must have been smaller and smaller.

William Lane Craig further explains, "As you trace this expansion back in time, the universe grows denser and denser and denser until finally, the entire known universe is concentrated down to a state of infinite density that would mark the beginning of the universe. At this point, which cosmologists call the 'singularity,' all matter and energy — physical space and time themselves — came into being. This literally represents the origin of the universe from nothing."

Do you think it is reasonable to conclude that if the universe is, in fact, continually expanding, then at earlier points in its history it must have been smaller and denser, to such an extent that the entire known universe began from a single point of infinite density called a "singularity"? Can you think of another viable theory behind the continual expansion of the universe? Give reasons for your answer.

"The most reasonable belief is that we came from nothing, by nothing, and for nothing."

Atheist Quentin Smith

5. According to Stephen Hawking, "Almost everyone now believes that the universe, and time itself, had a beginning at the Big Bang." When did you first become familiar with the so-called Big Bang theory? What was your initial opinion of the theory at that time?

"Set aside the many competing explanations of the Big Bang; something made an entire cosmos out of nothing. It is this realization—that something transcendent started it all—which has hard-science types ... using terms like 'miracle.'"
Journalist Gregg Easterbrook

Think About This!

Empirical Data for the Big Bang

"In the 1920s, the Russian mathematician Alexander Friedman and the [Belgian] astronomer George Lemaître were able to develop models based on Einstein's theory. They predicted the universe was expanding. Of course, this meant that if you went backward in time, the universe would go back to a single origin before which it didn't exist. Astronomer Fred Hoyle derisively called this the Big Bang—and the name stuck!

"In 1929, the American astronomer Edwin Hubble discovered that the light coming to us from distant galaxies appears to be redder than it should be, and that this is a universal feature of galaxies in all parts of the sky. Hubble explained

this red shift as being due to the fact that the galaxies are moving away from us. He concluded that the universe is literally flying apart at enormous velocities.

"In the 1940s, George Gamow predicted that if the Big Bang really happened, then the background temperature of the universe should be just a few degrees above absolute zero.... Sure enough, in 1965, two scientists accidentally discovered the universe's background radiation — and it was only about 3.7 degrees above absolute zero.

"Predictions about the Big Bang have been consistently verified by scientific data. Moreover, they have been corroborated by the failure of every attempt to falsify them by alternative models. Unquestionably, the Big Bang model has impressive scientific credentials."

William Lane Craig

6. In your opinion, how probable is it that the Big Bang model is correct and before the universe existed there was nothing?

"It's important to understand how reversed the situation is from a hundred years ago. Back then, Christians had to maintain by faith in the Bible that despite all appearances to the contrary, the universe was not eternal but was created out of nothing a finite time ago. Now the situation is exactly the opposite."

William Lane Craig

Optional Discussion Questions

- How much of the related chapter in *The Case for a Creator* were you able to read? What impacted you most?

- Does it take more faith to accept that the universe had no cause or to accept that there had to be a First Cause to all that exists?

- What's the difference, if any, between an expanding universe and an evolving universe?

- Do you believe the universe is expanding and will continue to expand indefinitely? Is that compatible with the world around you as you experience it? Why or why not?

- Which do you prefer: a static universe with everything in its proper place or an expanding universe with everything out of control, but enjoying the ride? Explain.

WATCH THIS!

DVD Teaching Segment #2

"In three minutes, 98 percent of all matter there is or will ever be has been produced. We have a universe. It is a place of the most wondrous and gratifying possibility, and beautiful, too. And it was all done in about the time it takes to make a sandwich."
Bill Bryson, *A Short History of Nearly Everything*

DISCUSS THIS!

7. The *kalam* cosmological argument provides three simple steps to a line of reasoning for God's existence: (1) whatever begins to exist has a cause; (2) the universe began to exist; (3) therefore, the universe has a cause.

    Do you agree with the deductive reasoning behind the *kalam* argument? Why or why not? If not, where do you believe the argument falls apart?

"Since an infinite past would involve an actually infinite number of events, then the past simply can't be infinite, and the universe must have had a beginning."

William Lane Craig

NOTE: In *The Case for a Creator* (pages 108 – 112), William Lane Craig demonstrates logically from the evidence that the Creator must be an uncaused, beginningless, timeless, spaceless, immaterial, personal being endowed with freedom of will and enormous power—all unmistakable attributes of the divine.

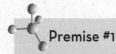 ## Premise #1

Whatever begins to exist has a cause.

"We certainly have empirical evidence for the truth of this premise. This is a principle that is constantly confirmed and never falsified. We never see things coming into being uncaused out of nothing."

William Lane Craig

"I never asserted so absurd a proposition as that anything might arise without a cause."

Renowned skeptic David Hume (1754)

8. William Lane Craig states, "It seems metaphysically necessary that any-thing which *begins* to exist *has* to have a cause that brings it into being. Things don't just pop into existence, uncaused, out of nothing. The idea that things can come into being uncaused out of nothing is worse than magic. At least when a magician pulls a rabbit out of a hat, there's the magician and the hat!"

How convincing is the first premise of the *kalam* cosmological argu-ment — that whatever begins to exist has a cause? Do you agree with Craig's statement? Is this the most rational view? Why or why not? Can you think of any exceptions to this rule? What reasons support this premise to be either true or false?

Premise #2

The universe began to exist.

"In the beginning there was an explosion. Not an explosion like those familiar on Earth, starting from a definite center and spreading out to engulf more and more of the circumambient air, but an explosion which occurred simultaneously every-where, filling all space from the beginning with every particle of matter rushing apart from every other particle."

Physicist Steven Weinberg,
The First Three Minutes

9. Early Christian and Muslim scholars used mathematical reasoning to demonstrate that it was impossible to have an infinite past. Their conclusion, therefore, was that the universe's age must be finite — that is, it must have had a beginning. The second premise of the *kalam* argument says that the universe began to exist.

   Do you think the evidence from mathematics and cosmology sufficiently supports this claim that the universe had a beginning at some point in the past? Why or why not? Do you agree that the universe can't have an infinite number of actual events in its past; and it therefore must have had a beginning? Why or why not?

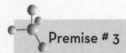

Premise # 3

Therefore, the universe has a cause.

"In atheism, the universe just pops into being out of nothing, with absolutely no explanation at all. I think once people understand the concept of absolute nothingness, it's simply obvious to them that if something has a beginning, that it could not have popped into being out of nothing but must have a cause that brings it into existence."

William Lane Craig

10. The *kalam* argument says that if its first two premises are true, then it's necessary to conclude that the universe has a cause. Do you agree or disagree that this is the only logical conclusion? Why or why not?

11. It is one thing to state that the universe has a cause, and quite another thing to claim that fact leads to theological implications. How big of a leap is it to deduce that since the universe has a cause, that cause must therefore be a divine being? Explain.

"Even atheist Kai Nielson said, 'Suppose you suddenly hear a loud bang ... and you ask me, "What made that bang?" and I reply, "Nothing, it just happened." You would not accept that.' He's right, of course. And if a cause is needed for a small bang like that, then it's needed for the Big Bang as well."

William Lane Craig

Think About This!

"If everything must have a cause, then the First Cause must be caused and there-fore: Who made God? To say that this First Cause always existed is to deny the basic assumption of this theory."

David Marshall Brooks, *The Necessity of Atheism*

"I never said everything must have a cause. The premise is that whatever begins to exist must have a cause. In other words, 'being' can't come from 'nonbeing.' Since God never began to exist [that is, he never had a beginning], he doesn't require a cause. He never came into being.... Atheists themselves used to be very comfortable in maintaining that the universe is eternal and uncaused. The prob-lem is that they can no longer hold that position because of modern evidence that the universe started with the Big Bang. So they can't legitimately object when I make the same claim about God—he is eternal and he is uncaused."

William Lane Craig

12. Atheist George Smith states, "If *everything* must have a cause, how did God become exempt?" How would you respond to Smith's question?

13. Theoretical physicist Stephen Hawking said, "We are such insignificant creatures on a minor planet of a very average star in the outer suburbs of one of a hundred thousand million galaxies. So it is difficult to believe in a God that would care about us or even notice our existence." Do you agree? Why or why not? Why is it difficult to believe in a God who would notice and care about us?

Optional Discussion Questions

• Christians often caution that a skeptic cannot be argued into faith. Yet if someone were sincerely open-minded, could the *kalam* cosmological argument be sufficient to prompt a verdict in favor of a supernatural Creator? Or would it merely become fodder for more and more creative — or, as some might say, desperate — counterarguments and objections?

• Is God dead? Is it possible that a Creator put the universe in motion, but later ceased to exist? How would you formulate a response to this possibility?

• William Lane Craig suggests that God is personal. What does that mean? Define "personal creator." How would this be different from "The Force" of *Star Wars*? What are some of the implications for us if God is personal?

WATCH THIS!

DVD Wrap-up/Lee's Perspective

In which direction—toward a Creator, or away from one—do you think the current arrow of cosmology is pointing? What piece of evidence is most influencing your answer at this point?

"There is a kind of religion in science; it is the religion of a person who believes there is order and harmony in the Universe. Every event can be explained in a rational way as the product of some previous event; every effect must have its cause; there is no First Cause.... This religious faith of the scientist is violated by the discovery that the world had a beginning under conditions in which the known laws of physics are not valid, and as a product of forces or circumstances we cannot discover. When that happens, the scientist has lost control. If he really examined the implications, he would be traumatized."

Astronomer Robert Jastrow

BETWEEN SESSIONS

Personal Reflection

*In the beginning God created the heavens and the earth. Now the earth
was formless and empty, darkness was over the surface of the deep, and
the Spirit of God was hovering over the waters. And God said, "Let there be
light," and there was light. God saw that the light was good.*

Genesis 1:1–4a

- Carefully read the Genesis account above, then compare and contrast this description with what you understand science has discovered regarding the origin of the universe. In what ways does this 3,500-year-old passage align with the Big Bang theory?

- Think about the universe and how vast, incredible, and awe-inspiring it is. How unbelievable is it to you that the chain of events leading to your life in this very moment—all matter, space, and even time—originated instantaneously out of nothing, in a flash of light and energy?

- Thousands of years ago, the Hebrews believed everything began with the primordial *fiat lux*—the voice of God commanding light into existence. Do you believe that something as expansive as the universe could have come out of absolutely nothing? How much of a stretch is it for you to consider the possibility that a divine Creator has always existed and caused that moment to occur? To what extent does this claim, regardless of its source, require you to take a leap of faith?

- The biblical book of Hebrews (11:1–3) teaches, "Now faith is being sure of what we hope for and certain of what we do not see. This is what the ancients were commended for. By faith we understand that the universe was formed at God's command, so that what is seen was not made out of what was visible." Think about some examples of things you are sure of, but you cannot actually see. If faith is being certain of what cannot be seen, what do you currently have faith in?

- If you'd like, take a few moments to sincerely acknowledge your doubts about the origin of the universe with a simple, honest prayer. If God is real and has the power to create something as spectacular as billions of galaxies, wouldn't he also have the power to help you increase your faith? Why not suspend your disbelief for the moment and give God an opportunity to respond to you?

THE FINE-TUNING
OF THE UNIVERSE

It's turning out that the Earth is anything but ordinary, that our sun is far from average, and that even the position of our planet in the galaxy is eerily fortuitous. The idea that the universe is a flourishing hothouse of advanced civilizations is now being undermined by surprising new scientific discoveries and fresh thinking.... Whichever way I looked, the inference of design seemed inescapable. If ours is the only universe in existence, which is a logical conclusion based on the evidence, then its highly sophisticated fine-tuning cries out for a designer.

Lee Strobel, *The Case for a Creator*

READ THIS!

If possible, read the following content in preparation for your group meeting. Otherwise, read it as follow-up.

The Case for a Creator, chapter 6: The Evidence of Physics

The Case for a Creator, chapter 7: The Evidence of Astronomy

Or, *The Case for a Creator Student Edition*, chapter 4: The Cosmos on a Razor's Edge

WATCH THIS!

DVD Teaching Segment #1

For every DVD clip, space is provided to take notes on anything that stands out to you.

DISCUSS THIS!

1. Quick—go around your group! Does the universe appear to be planned or unplanned to you?

"The fine-tuning of the physical laws and constants of the universe and the precise configuration of its initial conditions, dating back to the very origin of the universe itself, suggest the need for a cause that's intelligent."

Science philosopher
Stephen C. Meyer

Think About This!

"Imagine a ruler, or one of those old-fashioned linear radio dials, that goes all the way across the universe. It would be broken down into one-inch increments, which means there would be billions upon billions upon billions of inches. The entire dial represents the range of force strengths in nature, with gravity being the weakest force and the strong nuclear force that binds protons and neutrons together in the nuclei being the strongest, a whopping ten thousand billion billion billion billion times stronger than gravity. The range of possible settings for the force of gravity can plausibly be taken to be at least as large as the total range of force strengths. Now, let's imagine that you want to move the dial from where it's currently set. Even if you were to move it by only one inch, the impact on life in the universe would be catastrophic.... Animals anywhere near the size of human beings would be crushed."

Robin Collins

2. To what extent does the example of the precision of the force of gravity add weight to the argument that the universe was designed?

"It is hard to resist the impression that the present structure of the universe, apparently so sensitive to minor alterations in numbers, has been rather carefully thought out.... The seemingly miraculous concurrence of these numerical values must remain the most compelling evidence for cosmic design."
Physicist Paul Davies

Think About This!

"The cosmological constant (the expansion speed of space in the universe), which is part of Einstein's equation for General Relativity, could have had any value, positive or negative. If large and positive, the cosmological constant would act as a repulsive force that increases with distance, a force that would prevent matter from clumping together in the early universe, the process that was the first step in forming galaxies and stars and planets and people. If large and negative, the cosmological constant would act as an attractive force increasing with distance, a force that would almost immediately reverse the expansion of the universe and cause it to recollapse. In fact, astronomical observations show that the cosmological constant is quite small, very much smaller than would have been guessed from first principles."

Nobel Prize – winning physicist Steven Weinberg

3. If the universe were put on trial for a charge of having been designed, and the fine-tuning of the cosmological constant and the force of gravity were the only evidence introduced, would you vote "guilty" or "not guilty"? Elaborate.

"It is quite easy to understand why so many scientists have changed their minds in the past thirty years, agreeing that the universe cannot reasonably be explained as a cosmic accident. Evidence for an intelligent designer becomes more compelling the more we understand our carefully crafted habitat."

Scientist Walter Bradley

Think About This!

"The fine-tuning of the universe refers to the extraordinary balancing of the fundamental laws and parameters of physics and the initial conditions of the universe. Our minds can't comprehend the precision of some of them. The result is a universe that has just the right conditions to sustain life. The coincidences are simply too amazing to have been the result of happenstance. Over the past thirty years or so, scientists have discovered that just about everything about the basic structure of the universe is balanced on a razor's edge for life to exist."

Robin Collins

There are more than thirty separate parameters that require precise calibration in order to produce a life-sustaining universe, including:

- *Gravitational force*
- *Electromagnetic force*
- *Strong nuclear force*
- *Weak nuclear force*
- *Speed of light*
- *Planck's constant*
- *Proton mass*
- *Electron mass*
- *Cosmological constant*
- *Mass density of the universe*
- *Carlson energy resonance*
- *Water*
- *Original phase-space volume*
- *Galactic Habitable Zone*

- *26 essential elements required for human life*
- *Earth's composition of elements*
- *A spiral galaxy (and Earth's location in it)*
- *A circular orbit*
- *Surrounding planets*
- *Circumstellar Habitable Zone*
- *An uncommon sun—yellow dwarf star*
- *A large moon*
- *The mass (size) of the earth*
- *Oxygen-rich atmosphere (20 percent)*
- *Plate tectonics*
- *The earth's albedo (reflectivity)*

4. If a Creator really does exist, would you expect the universe to be deliberate and directed or random and undirected? Elaborate.

5. Can you think of ways to try to explain away the universe's fine-tuning? How well do those alternative explanations deal with the evidence?

"Uncovering the laws of physics resembles completing a crossword [puzzle] in a number of ways.... In the case of the crossword, it would never occur to us to suppose that the words just happened to fall into a consistent interlocking pattern by accident."

Paul Davies

6. Paul Davies asks, "If the world's finest minds can unravel only with difficulty the deeper workings of nature, how could it be supposed that those workings are merely a mindless accident, a product of blind chance?" How would you respond to his question?

Can luck really explain why the Earth enjoys this incredible convergence of extremely unlikely circumstances that have allowed human beings to flourish? Explain.

7. Astronomer George Greenstein asks, "Is it possible that suddenly, without intending to, we have stumbled upon scientific proof of the existence of a Supreme Being? Was it God who stepped in and so providentially crafted the cosmos for our benefit?" What do you think?

"An honest man, armed with all the knowledge available to us now, could only state that in some sense, the origin of life appears at the moment to be almost a miracle, so many are the conditions which would have had to have been satisfied to get it going."
Nobel Prize winner Francis Crick

Optional Discussion Questions

- How much of the related chapters in *The Case for a Creator* were you able to read? What impacted you most?

- What are some examples of fine-tuning in everyday life — things that hang on the convergence of several variables? What are examples of outcomes that are *not* dependent on variables?

- Do you believe in "accidents," or is everything orchestrated? How does one tell the difference?

- In his book, *The Mind of God*, Paul Davies writes: "Through my scientific work I have come to believe more and more strongly that the physical universe is put together with an ingenuity so astonishing that I cannot accept it merely as brute fact. I cannot believe that our existence in the universe is a mere quirk of fate, an accident of history, an incidental blip in the great cosmic drama." Conversely, astronomer Carl Sagan writes: "There's nothing unusual about Earth. It's an average, unassuming rock that's spinning mindlessly around an unremarkable star in a run-of-the-mill galaxy — a lonely speck in the great enveloping cosmic dark." Do you believe that the universe has been put together with astonishing ingenuity or is our existence a quirk of fate? Is there anything special about our planet? Give reasons for your answers.

- Is it possible that the universe could have been more precisely tuned with a better outcome?

- Physicist Freeman Dyson was quoted in the *New York Times* as saying, "The universe in some sense must have known that we were coming." What do you think he meant by this statement? Does it appear probable or even possible to you that the laws of nature have been carefully arranged so that a Creator could be "discovered"? Or is there another explanation? Elaborate.

WATCH THIS!

DVD Teaching Segment #2

DISCUSS THIS!

8. How possible do you think it is that life exists in another galaxy? How would the existence of life elsewhere affect your spiritual views?

"The fact that life flourishes on our planet isn't exceptional. Creatures of all kinds undoubtedly abound, we're told, in countless locations among the ten trillion billion stars in the universe. Some scientists have estimated there are up to ten trillion advanced civilizations."
Carl Sagan

Think About This!

"The 'multiple universe' argument can be summarized this way: 'There could have been millions and millions of different universes, each created with different dial settings of the fundamental ratios and constants, so many in fact that the right set was bound to turn up by sheer chance. We just happen to be the lucky ones."

Robert Jastrow, *God and the Astronomers*

9.   What do you make of the theory of "multiple universes"? Do you think other universes exist? Can you cite any evidence for their existence? Do you agree that without a "multi-universe" theory the incredible fine-tuning of the universe points powerfully to an Intelligent Designer?

"There's no real reason to believe such parallel worlds exist. The very fact that skeptics have to come up with such an outlandish theory is because the fine-tuning of the universe points powerfully toward an intelligent designer — and some people will hypothesize anything to avoid reaching that conclusion."

William Lane Craig

10. In the DVD segment, Jay Richards states that the "multi-universe" theory is "an interesting idea, but there's really only one problem with it. There's no independent evidence that it's true. Besides, it really just pushes the question back a step because we could still ask who built the generator [that would be needed to produce the multiple universes]?"

If it could be substantiated that there are multiple universes in existence, does that increase or decrease the likelihood that our finely tuned universe was a product of chance? Why?

Think About This!

"You would need to make trillions upon trillions upon trillions upon trillions of universes in order to increase the odds that the cosmological constant would come out right at least once, since it's finely tuned to an incomprehensible degree. And that's just one parameter."

Robin Collins

"Regardless of which multiple-universe theory you use, in every case you'd need a 'many-universes generator'—and it would require the right structure, the right mechanism, and the right ingredients to churn out new universes. It's highly unlikely that such a universe-generating system would have all the right components in place by random chance, just like random chance can't account for how a bread-maker produces loaves of edible bread. So if a many-universe-generating system exists, there would still need to be an intelligent designer to make the finely tuned universe-generating process work."

Robin Collins

"The multiverse idea rests on assumptions that would be laughed out of town if they came from a religious text. The theory requires as much suspension of disbelief as any religion. Join the church that believes in the existence of invisible objects fifty billion galaxies wide!"

Journalist Gregg Easterbrook

Optional Discussion Questions

- To what degree does the belief in a Creator necessitate a belief that there are no other habitable planets other than Earth? In other words, if there is life beyond Earth, does this preclude the existence of God? Why or why not?

- Do you think it is necessary to collect hard evidence in order to conclude whether or not something is true? For example, just because we don't have evidence to support the multiple universe theory doesn't necessarily mean multiple universes don't exist. Do you agree or disagree? Why?

- How much evidence is required before you are willing to decide if something is true? Elaborate.

- Robin Collins explains that "though invoking God may not be strictly part of science, it is in the spirit of science to follow the evidence and its implications wherever they lead us." Do you agree that if the facts fit with a "God hypothesis," the field of science should be open to it?

"If there's only one universe, then the conclusion that the universe looks fine-tuned because it is fine-turned is inescapable. But if our universe is just one of a vast set, then you seem to have more resources to play with. Chance gets a new lease on life.

Jay Wesley Richards,
Discovery Institute

WATCH THIS!

DVD Wrap-up/Lee's Perspective

In which direction — toward a Creator, or away from one — do you think the current arrow of physics and fine-tuning is pointing? What piece of evidence is most influencing your answer at this point?

*"Science has discovered
that our existence is
infinitely improbable,
and hence a miracle."*
Science journalist
John Horgan

BETWEEN SESSIONS

Personal Reflection

> But ask the animals, and they will teach you,
>> or the birds of the air, and they will tell you;
> or speak to the earth, and it will teach you,
>> or let the fish of the sea inform you.
> Which of all these does not know
>> that the hand of the LORD has done this?
> In his hand is the life of every creature
>> and the breath of all mankind.
>
> Job 12:7–10 NIV

- The book of Job is considered to be the oldest book in the Bible, written in a poetic style to convey one man's experience with God. In the above verses, what does Job seem to believe about the Lord? What leads him to this conclusion?

- The more you learn of the astronomical odds of the incredible razor's-edge precision of the universe, how likely does the existence of a Creator become to you? What do the intricacies of creation reveal about the One who created it all? Describe what the Creator might be like.

- Later in the book of Job, God turns the tables and poses some very probing questions of his own! Read the following passage, imagining there is a God who holds the universe together and speaks directly to you. How would you respond?

> Then the LORD answered Job out of the storm. He said:
> "Who is this that darkens my counsel
>> with words without knowledge?
> Brace yourself like a man;
>> I will question you,
>> and you shall answer me.
> Where were you when I laid the earth's foundation?
>> Tell me, if you understand.
> Who marked off its dimensions? Surely you know!
>> Who stretched a measuring line across it?
> On what were its footings set,
>> or who laid its cornerstone—

while the morning stars sang together
    and all the angels shouted for joy?
Who shut up the sea behind doors
    when it burst forth from the womb,
when I made the clouds its garment
    and wrapped it in thick darkness,
when I fixed limits for it
    and set its doors and bars in place,
when I said, 'This far you may come and no farther;
    here is where your proud waves halt'?
Have you ever given orders to the morning,
    or shown the dawn its place,…
Have you comprehended the vast expanses of the earth?
    Tell me, if you know all this."

Job 38:1–12, 18 NIV

• In addition to the poetic beauty of these words, how are these questions still relevant today, despite all of the scientific progress people have made? How do the questions God poses impact you? Consider how God accuses Job of speaking "words without knowledge." As much as we've learned about the cosmos since the days of Job, shouldn't we humbly admit how much knowledge we still lack and how powerless we really are in the vast scheme of things? It's really true: "The more we've learned, the less we know!"

• Is it possible that humankind will someday *know* everything? What are the implications of your answer? Can we ever become equal to the One who "laid the earth's foundation"? Will we ever have the power to "give orders to the morning, or show the dawn its place"? What do you believe about our ultimate potential and limitations?

• In what ways is God speaking to you at this moment through your observations of creation and his words from the Bible? Reread Job 38:1–12, 18 and then respond sincerely to him in your own words. Remember that God invites you to talk to him freely and openly! He welcomes your honesty and your doubts. And he just may have some answers for you too, if you're listening.

THE EVIDENCE
OF BIOCHEMISTRY

So far, the evidence from the telescope to the microscope was pointing powerfully in the direction of a Creator — a circumstance I never would have dreamed possible back in my days as a student. I was left with an urgent desire to continue my investigation. Still, I also was experiencing an underlying skepticism. Would the case for a Creator hold up when it was scrutinized more carefully and when I could cross-examine experts with all of the questions that plagued me?

Lee Strobel, *The Case for a Creator*

READ THIS!

If possible, read the following content in preparation for your group meeting. Otherwise, read it as follow-up.

The Case for a Creator, chapter 8: The Evidence of Biochemistry

Or, *The Case for a Creator Student Edition*, chapter 5: Mousetraps and Molecular Machines

WATCH THIS!

DVD Teaching Segment #1

For every DVD clip, space is provided to take notes on anything that stands out to you.

DISCUSS THIS!

1. What's your reaction to the fact that a eukaryotic cell, the basic unit of life, is a complicated molecular machine, a tenth of the size of the head of a pin, made up of about three billion units of DNA?

"We have always under-estimated the cell.... The entire cell can be viewed as a factory that contains an elaborate network of interlocking assembly lines, each of which is composed of a set of large protein machines."

Bruce Alberts, president, National Academy of Sciences

2. Consider the bacterial flagellum described in the video. Do you agree with Michael Behe that the parts of this machine could not have been assembled by chance? Why or why not?

Think About This!

"The flagellum's propeller can spin at ten thousand revolutions per minute. As a car aficionado, I was staggered by that statistic! A friend had recently given me a ride in his exotic high-performance sports car, and I knew it wasn't capable of generating that many rpms. Even the notoriously high-revving Honda S2000, with a state-of-the-art, four-cylinder, two-liter, dual-overhead-cam aluminum block engine, featuring four valves per cylinder and variable intake and exhaust valve timing, has a redline of only nine thousand rpms."

Lee Strobel

3. Howard Berg of Harvard has labeled the flagellum "the most efficient machine in the universe." Indeed, biologists agree it's more efficient than any machine humankind has ever produced — especially on its microscopic scale. Do you think we will ever be able to build something more efficient? Why or why not? If that breakthrough were ever to occur, would that impact your assessment of the flagellum?

Think About This!

"One scientist described a single-cell organism as a high-tech factory, complete with artificial languages and their decoding systems, memory banks for information storage and retrieval, elegant control systems regulating the automated assembly of parts and components, error fail-safe and proof-reading devices utilized for quality control, assembly processes involving the principle of prefabrication and modular construction … and a capacity not equaled in any of our own most advanced machines, for it would be capable of replicating its entire structure within a matter of a few hours."

Franklin M. Harold, *The Way of the Cell*

4. What do you think accounts for the remarkable complexity and apparent design of the microscopic machinery contained within the cell?

"Most scientists speculated that the deeper they delved into the cell, the more simplicity they would find. But the opposite happened."

Biochemist Michael Behe,
Lehigh University

5. Michael Behe claims that Darwinism was a lot more plausible when we
    were thinking of cells in terms of globs of protoplasm (like gelatin) rather
    than molecular machines. Do you agree or disagree with Behe's assess-
    ment? Explain.

---

*"A flagellum is on the order of a couple of microns. A
micron is about 1/20,000 of an inch. Most of its length
is the propeller. The motor itself would be maybe
1/100,000ths of an inch. Even with all of our technology,
we can't even begin to create something like this."*
Michael Behe

Fast Fact

Biochemistry: *The study of the chemical characteristics and reactions of particu-
lar living organisms or biological substances*
Microbiology: *A branch of biology dealing particularly with microscopic forms
of life*
Nanotechnology: *The art of manipulating materials on an atomic or molecular
scale especially to build microscopic devices*

Optional Discussion Questions

- How much of the related chapter in *The Case for a Creator* were you able to read? What impacted you most?

- As scientists peer deeper and deeper into the workings of cells, do you believe they will find more or less complexity? How might this influence your opinion about whether the cell is designed or the product of evolutionary development?

- The video clip stated that "biochemical machines are a masterpiece of engineering and nanotechnology and are essential to functions as vital and diverse as vision, photosynthesis, and the production of energy in the cell." Is the word "masterpiece" the best descriptor of the biochemical machines? How would you describe these machines? In what ways might they *not* be a masterpiece of engineering and nanotechnology?

- How do you feel about the idea that your body is basically comprised of millions of microscopic machines? How does this fact change how you view yourself?

- In what ways are we machine-like? What distinguishes humans from machines or animals?

WATCH THIS!

DVD Teaching Segment #2

DISCUSS THIS!

6. "Irreducible complexity" is a phrase coined by biochemist Michael Behe that says: *multi-component parts of certain organelles, or systems within a cell, are all necessary for function, and the removal of one part causes the function of the system to be lost.* Restate this definition in your own words. What questions does it raise for you?

Think About This!

"A system or device is irreducibly complex if it has a number of different components that all work together to accomplish the task of the system, and if you were to remove one of the components, the system would no longer function. An irreducibly complex system is highly unlikely to be built piece-by-piece through

Darwinian processes, because the system has to be fully present in order for it to function.

"The illustration I like to use is a mousetrap. If you take away any one of the parts — the spring or the holding bar or whatever — then it's not like the mousetrap becomes half as efficient as it used to be or it only catches half as many mice. Instead, it doesn't catch any mice. It's broken. It doesn't work at all."

Michael Behe

7. Do you agree with Behe's conclusion that it is impossible to put an irreducibly complex organism together gradually and, at the same time, maintain its functionality at each successive step? Why or why not?

"If the creation of a simple device like [the mousetrap] requires intelligent design, then we have to ask, 'What about the finely tuned machines of the cellular world?' If evolution can't adequately explain them, then scientists should be free to consider other alternatives."

Michael Behe

Think About This!

"Evolution can't produce an irreducibly complex biological machine suddenly, all at once, because it's much too complicated. The odds against that would be prohibitive. And you can't produce it directly by numerous, successive, slight modifications of a precursor system, because any precursor system would be missing a part and consequently couldn't function. There would be no reason for it to exist. And natural selection chooses systems that are already working."

Michael Behe

"Genetic studies have shown that between thirty and thirty-five proteins are needed to create a functional flagellum. I haven't even begun to describe all of its complexities; we don't even know the roles of all its proteins. But at a minimum you need at least three parts — a paddle, a rotor, and a motor — that are made up of various proteins. Eliminate one of those parts and you don't get a flagellum that only spins at five thousand rpms; you get a flagellum that simply doesn't work at all. So it's irreducibly complex — and a huge stumbling block to Darwinian theory."

Michael Behe

8. How does the irreducibly complex cell potentially pose a problem for Darwin's theory that all living systems have been formed by numerous, successive, slight modifications over time by natural selection? Elaborate.

9. Charles Darwin wrote in *The Origin of Species*, "If it could be demonstrated that any complex organ existed which could not possibly have been formed by numerous, successive, slight modifications, my theory would absolutely break down." Does Darwin's theory pass or fail his own test for the evolution of irreducibly complex systems? Explain.

10. If Darwin were alive today, do you think he would continue to support his own theory? Why or why not?

"Right now, there's only one principle that we know can come up with complex interactive systems, and that's intelligence."

Michael Behe

11. Do you think it's legitimate for scientists to consider the possibility of an Intelligent Designer if the evidence points in that direction? Why or why not?

Optional Discussion Questions

- In the DVD segment, Michael Behe compares the flagellum to an outboard motor. If a tornado were to blow through a metal factory, what do you think the odds are that an outboard motor could ever get assembled by chance? Is it even possible? Likewise, without the intervention of some kind of intelligence, what are the odds for the chance assemblage of a single flagellum?

- In your opinion, has it been sufficiently demonstrated that the bacterial flagellum could not have been formed by numerous, successive, slight modifications? What is required to sufficiently demonstrate such a condition?

- Is "Intelligent Design" the only way, or one of many ways, to explain the origin of complex systems such as a mousetrap, an outboard motor, or a cell? Elaborate.

- How might new discoveries of the cell impact your view of a Creator?

WATCH THIS!

DVD Wrap-up/Lee's Perspective

In which direction — toward a Creator, or away from one — do you think the current arrow of biochemistry and biological machines is pointing? What piece of evidence is most influencing your answer at this point?

BETWEEN SESSIONS

Personal Reflection

> For you created my inmost being;
>   you knit me together in my mother's womb.
> I praise you because I am fearfully and wonderfully made;
>   your works are wonderful,
>   I know that full well.
> My frame was not hidden from you
>   when I was made in the secret place.
>
>   Psalm 139:13 – 15a NIV

- What have you discovered in this session that has surprised or impacted you the most? Is it the factory-like complexity of a single cell? The motor-like design of the bacterial flagellum? Or is it the realization that your own body is made up of millions of these microscopic machines?

- What do you think accounts for the remarkable complexity and design of this microscopic machinery? Is it Darwinian natural selection or is it possible that some kind of intelligent mind was the engineer?

- According to the Psalm 139:13–15a, what does the Bible claim is God's role in the creation of human life? With all you've discovered about the intricacies of the cell, do you have a new level of appreciation for how you've been so ingeniously "knit together"? Would you agree that the human body, even at the microscopic level, has been "fearfully and wonderfully made"?

- Psalm 139 is a song of praise for the mastermind behind it all—the Lord of all creation! Do you feel humbled or awed as you look more deeply into God's works? Reconsider the words Francis Collins, director of the Human Genome Project, quoted earlier in this guide: "We human scientists have an opportunity to understand the elegance and wisdom of God's creation in a way that is truly exhilarating. When a scientist discovers something that no human knew before, but God did—that is both an occasion for scientific excitement and, for a believer, also an occasion for worship."

- Do you feel exhilarated or excited by these glimpses into the ingenious mind of the Creator? Read the Psalm passage again. At this point in your spiritual journey, do you feel any sense of awe or even praise for God? If so, why don't you open your heart and speak to him about it at this moment —who knows what else he might reveal to you?

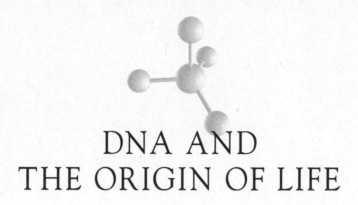

DNA AND
THE ORIGIN OF LIFE

Going far back into time, Christians have reached a far different conclusion: Earth was created by God as the stage upon which the human drama would be played out. What's amazing about modern science, including new discoveries just within the last few years, is that this view of the universe seems to be far better supported today than in ancient times.... In hindsight, my materialistic philosophy had been built on a foundation that history has subsequently dismantled piece by piece.

Lee Strobel, *The Case for a Creator*

READ THIS!

If possible, read the following content in preparation for your group meeting. Otherwise, read it as follow-up.

The Case for a Creator, chapter 9: The Evidence of Biological Information

Or, *The Case for a Creator Student Edition*, chapter 6: DNA and the Origin of Life

WATCH THIS!

DVD Teaching Segment #1

For every DVD clip, space is provided to take notes on anything that stands out to you.

DISCUSS THIS!

1. Read the following definition of DNA and summarize in your own words the main role of DNA molecules. Does this definition make sense to you? Why or why not? What questions, if any, does this raise for you?

   Deoxyribonucleic acid (DNA) is a nucleic acid that contains the genetic instructions used in the development and functioning of all known living organisms. The main role of DNA molecules is the long-term storage of information. DNA is often compared to a set of blueprints, since it contains the instructions needed to construct other components of cells, such as proteins and RNA molecules. The DNA segments that carry this genetic information are called genes.

2. Where do you think the information contained in DNA comes from? How did it arise in the first place? Can you think of another source, besides intelligence, that is capable of producing information?

Einstein said, "God does not play dice." He was right. God plays Scrabble.
Philip Gold, Discovery Institute

 Think About This!

"We know from our experience that we can convey information with a twenty-six-letter alphabet, or twenty-two, or thirty — or even just two characters, like the zeros and ones used in the binary code in computers. One of the most extraordinary discoveries of the twentieth century is that DNA actually stores information — the detailed instructions for assembling proteins — in the form of a four-character digital code. The characters happen to be chemicals called adenine, guanine, cytosine, and thymine. Scientists represent them with the letters A, G, C, and T, and that's appropriate because they function as alphabetic characters in the genetic text. Properly arranging those four 'bases' will instruct the cell to build different sequences of amino acids, which are the building blocks of proteins. Different arrangements of characters yield different sequences of amino acids."
Stephen C. Meyer

3. Stephen Meyer asks, "Imagine trying to generate even a simple book by throwing Scrabble letters onto the floor. Or imagine closing your eyes and picking Scrabble letters out of a bag. Are you going to produce *Hamlet* in anything like the time of the known universe?" What do you think? How long would it take to toss Scrabble letters in the air and produce a simple book by chance? How long would it take to produce *Hamlet*? Now, how probable is it that random chance produced the libraries of information contained in DNA? Is this a fair analogy? Why or why not?

"DNA is more like a library. An organism accesses the information that it needs from DNA so it can build some of its critical components. In DNA, there are long lines of A, C, G, and T's that are precisely arranged in order to create protein structure and folding. To build one protein, you typically need 1,200 to 2,000 letters or bases — which is a lot of information."

Science philosopher
Stephen C. Meyer

 Think About This!

"Human DNA contains more organized information than the Encyclopædia Britannica. If the full text of the encyclopedia were to arrive in computer code from outer space, most people would regard this as proof of the existence of extraterrestrial intelligence. But when seen in nature, it is explained as the workings of random forces."

George Sim Johnson, *Did Darwin Get It Right?*

4. Read George Sim Johnson's quote on page 94. Do you agree that most people would attribute code from outer space to extraterrestrial intelligence, and yet at the same time attribute code from nature to random chance? What are some possible explanations for this inconsistency?

> *"The origin of information in DNA — which is necessary for life to begin — is best explained by an intelligent cause rather than any of the types of naturalistic causes that scientists typically use to explain biological phenomena."*
>
> Stephen C. Meyer

Think About This!

"Based on our uniform and repeated experience (which is the basis of all scientific reasoning about the past), there is only one known cause of information, and that cause is intelligence. Whether we're looking at a hieroglyphic inscription, a section of text in a book, or computer software, if you have information and you trace it back to its source, invariably you come to intelligence. Therefore, when you find information inscribed along the backbone of the DNA molecule in the cell, the most rational inference — based upon repeated experience — is that an intelligence of some kind played a role in the origin of that information.

Stephen C. Meyer

"We've seen that neither chance, nor chance combined with natural selection, nor self-organizational processes have the causal power to produce information. But we do know of one entity that does have the required causal powers to produce

information, and that's intelligence. Whenever you find a sequential arrangement that's complex and corresponds to an independent pattern or functional requirement, this kind of information is always the product of intelligence. Scientists in many fields recognize this connection between information and intelligence. When archaeologists discovered the Rosetta stone, they didn't think its inscriptions were the product of random chance or self-organizational processes. Obviously, the sequential arrangements of symbols was conveying information, and it was a reasonable assumption that intelligence created it. The same principle is true for DNA."

Stephen C. Meyer

5. If you were a teacher evaluating Stephen Meyer on how well he defended his thesis that DNA is best explained by an Intelligent Cause, what grade would you give him? What reasons would you give in defending that grade?

"This new realm of molecular genetics is where we see the most compelling evidence of design on the earth."

Biology professor
Dean Kenyon

Optional Discussion Questions

- How much of the related chapter in *The Case for a Creator* were you able to read? What impacted you most?

- If you had to choose one explanation or the other, do you believe it's more likely that life formed by chance or that it was designed? Why?

- To what extent does it appear that the laws of nature have been carefully arranged so that they can be discovered? Does this matter? Why or why not? What might be the significance behind this "discoverability factor"?

- Lee Strobel believes the implications of the scientific evidence are profound. He wonders if the information inside every cell in every living creature could be the signature of a Creator. What do you think? Is God's fingerprint or signature on every living thing? Do you agree with Lee's assessment? Why or why not?

WATCH THIS!

DVD Teaching Segment #2

"DNA is like a software program, only much more complex than anything we've ever devised."
Bill Gates, founder of Microsoft

DISCUSS THIS!

6. How willing have you been to pursue the evidence of science wherever it leads? What factors have most influenced the degree to which you've been willing to keep an open mind?

7. After considering and discussing the most recent scientific evidence in these sessions, do you think it is logical and rational, or illogical and irrational, to conclude that there is something divine behind creation? Elaborate.

"An honest man, armed with all the knowledge available to us now, could only state that in some sense, the origin of life appears at the moment to be almost a miracle, so many are the conditions which would have had to have been satisfied to get it going."

Nobel Prize - winning geneticist
Francis Crick

Think About This!

"When we look at the evidence from cosmology, physics, biology, and human consciousness, we find that theism has amazing explanatory scope and power. The existence of God explains this broad range of evidence more simply, adequately, and comprehensively than any other worldview, including its main competitors: naturalism or pantheism. And the discovery of corroborating or supportive evidence is accelerating."

Stephen C. Meyer

8. Is God real? What do you believe right now about the existence of a Creator?

"God is merely a comforting myth."
Paleontologist
Stephen Jay Gould

Think About This!

"One of the most interesting things I've learned as I've gone on this journey of scientific discovery has been that you don't have to commit intellectual suicide to acknowledge the existence of an Intelligent Designer, because today science is pointing more directly toward a Creator than at any time in the history of the world."

Lee Strobel

9. What can science tell us about the nature of a Creator—his qualities, his attributes, his priorities? What *can't* it tell us? What are some other ways a Creator might make himself known? What are other reliable sources of information that could be pursued in investigating God?

"This most beautiful system of the sun, planets and comets could only proceed from the counsel and dominion of an intelligent and powerful Being."

Sir Isaac Newton

Think About This!

"The best data we have [concerning the origin of the universe] are exactly what I would have predicted, had I nothing to go on but the five books of Moses, the Psalms, and the Bible as a whole."

Nobel Prize–winning physicist Arno Penzias

"Ironically, the picture of the universe bequeathed to us by the most advanced twentieth-century science is closer in spirit to the vision presented in ... Genesis than anything offered by science since Copernicus."

Atheist-turned-Christian Patrick Glynn,
in *God: The Evidence*

"The exquisite order displayed by our scientific understanding of the physical world calls for the divine."

Vera Kistiakowski, professor emeritus of physics,
Massachusetts Institute of Technology

"People see God every day, they just don't recognize him."

Pearl Bailey

"It is only through the supernatural that I can understand the mystery of existence."

Cosmologist Allan Sandage

"From a knowledge of God's work we shall know him."

Robert Boyle, father of modern chemistry

Optional Discussion Questions

- Physicist Paul Davies concludes that the universe has been together with astonishing ingenuity. Do you agree with Davies' conclusion? Why or why not? What about things like "black holes" that gobble up other celestial bodies? Why would something like this have been designed?

- If the evidence of science points toward a Creator, then where does faith fit in? In other words, what's the interplay between facts and faith?

- What are the pros and cons of a world with or without God?

- If you are convinced that a Creator does exist, to what extent do you think it's possible to have a personal relationship with him? To what degree do you want to know and experience God? What might this relational experience be like for you?

"I cannot imagine how the clockwork of the universe can exist without a clockmaker."
Voltaire

WATCH THIS!

DVD Wrap-up/Lee's Perspective

As you conclude this curriculum, in which direction—toward a Creator, or away from one—do you think the current arrow of science is pointing? What piece of evidence is most influencing your answer at this point:

IN THE COMING DAYS

Personal Reflection

> The heavens declare the glory of God;
> the skies proclaim the work of his hands.
> Day after day they pour forth speech;
> night after night they display knowledge.
> They have no speech, they use no words;
> no sound is heard from them.
> Yet their voice goes out into all the earth,
> their words to the ends of the world.

Psalm 19:1–4a

- What is your immediate reaction to the above Bible verses? What do you think the ancient author of this psalm was trying to express? What is meant by the words, "Day after day they pour forth speech; night after night they display knowledge"? Do you agree that the heavens declare the handiwork of a Creator, that this kind of "speech" supercedes cultural and language barriers?

- Is the author of the psalm indifferent to the expanse of the universe or is he awed by it? Can you relate to his sentiments about the world around you in any way? How do *you* feel when you look into the night sky on a clear evening and see a pattern of distant suns or the full round moon hanging low and large on the horizon?

- Has your sense of wonder been in any way reinvigorated by your study and discussion of *The Case for a Creator*? If so, what has impacted you most? Is it the scientific community's doubts about Darwinism? The evidence that the universe had a finite beginning just as the Bible has always stated all along? The incredible fine-tuning and razor's-edge precision within which all life hangs in the balance? The intricate and irreducibly complex nature of a "simple cell"? Or the discovery of the vast libraries of information stored in DNA — the complicated language of life? Has your belief system been in any way challenged as you've read, listened, questioned, and discussed the most recent scientific discoveries that show how improbable and miraculous life really is?

- Romans 1:20 says, "For since the creation of the world God's invisible qualities — his eternal power and divine nature — have been clearly seen, being understood from what has been made, so that people are without excuse." In what ways have you seen the fingerprints of God at work in creation? How has your opinion changed recently? How much more evidence of God's invisible qualities do we have today than the author of Romans had?

- If you're willing, take some time now to talk to the God who created and sustains it all. If you feel ready, you could even invite this great and powerful God into your life. Start by praying something like, "I don't know very much about you, but I believe you're real and you're powerful, and you can do anything. Please come into my life and teach me. Forgive me for ignoring you in any way and help me to know you more." If you pray a prayer like this with sincerity, the God of the Bible promises he will answer you.

The Case for Christ

A Six-Session Investigation of the Evidence for Jesus

Lee Strobel and Garry Poole

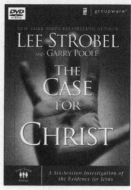

Is there credible evidence that Jesus of Nazareth really is the Son of God?

Retracing his own spiritual journey from atheism to faith, Lee Strobel, former legal editor of the *Chicago Tribune*, cross-examines several experts with doctorates from schools like Cambridge, Princeton, and Brandeis who are recognized authorities in their own fields.

- Strobel challenges them with questions like:
- How reliable is the New Testament?
- Does evidence for Jesus exist outside the Bible?
- Is there any reason to believe the resurrection was an actual event?

Strobel's tough, point-blank questions make this six-session video study a captivating, fast-paced experience. But it's not fiction. It's a riveting quest for the truth about history's most compelling figure.

6 sessions; 1 DVD with leader's guide, 90 minutes (approximate).

A *Case for Christ* participant's guide also available separately.

DVD-ROM 978-0-310-28280-8
Participant's Guide 978-0-310-28282-2

Pick up a copy today at your favorite bookstore!

ZondervanGroupware™ Small Group Edition

Faith Under Fire™ 1: Faith & Jesus

Four sessions on Jesus,
the Resurrection, Universalism,
and the Supernatural

with Lee Strobel

This cutting-edge curriculum features spirited discussions between well-respected Christians, people of other faiths, or people with no faith at all on important spiritual and social issues. Host Lee Strobel, best-selling author of *The Case for Christ* and *The Case for Faith*, provides additional comments to guide small group discussion.

Guests include: Rick Warren, Joni Eareckson Tada, Randy Alcorn, William Lane Craig, J. P. Moreland, Tony Campolo, and more.

Each volume contains a four-session DVD and leader's guide, and is intended to be used in conjunction with a corresponding participant's guide (sold separately).

Also in this series:

- Faith Under Fire 2: Faith & Facts
  Four sessions on the Bible, heaven, hell, and science
- Faith Under Fire 3: Tough Faith Questions
  Four sessions on forgiveness, pain and suffering, the Trinity, and Islam
- Faith Under Fire 4: A New Kind of Faith
  Four sessions on the relevance of Christianity

DVD 978-0-310-26828-4
Participant's Guide 978-0-310-26829-1

Pick up a copy today at your favorite bookstore!

The Case for the Real Jesus

A Journalist Investigates Current Attacks on the Identity of Christ

Lee Strobel, New York Times Bestselling Author

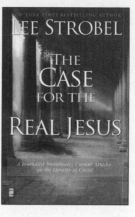

Has modern scholarship debunked the traditional Christ? Has the church suppressed the truth about Jesus to advance its own agenda? What if the real Jesus is far different from the atoning Savior worshipped through the centuries?

In *The Case for the Real Jesus*, former award-winning legal editor Lee Strobel explores such hot-button questions as:

- Did the church suppress ancient non-biblical documents that paint a more accurate picture of Jesus than the four Gospels?
- Did the church distort the truth about Jesus by tampering with early New Testament texts?
- Do new insights and explanations finally disprove the resurrection?
- Have fresh arguments disqualified Jesus from being the Messiah?
- Did Christianity steal its core ideas from earlier mythology?

Evaluate the arguments and evidence being advanced by prominent atheists, liberal theologians, Muslim scholars, and others. Sift through expert testimony. Then reach your own verdict in *The Case for the Real Jesus*.

Hardcover, Jacketed 978-0-310-24210-9

Pick up a copy today at your favorite bookstore!

Becoming a Contagious Christian

Six Sessions on Communicating Your Faith in a Style That Fits You

Mark Mittelberg, Lee Strobel, and Bill Hybels

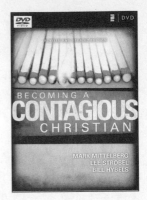

Over one million people have experienced the groundbreaking evangelism training course *Becoming a Contagious Christian*—a proven resource designed to equip believers for relational evangelism. Now **revised and updated**, it avoids stereotyped approaches that feel intimidating to many Christians—and to their friends! Instead, it shows ordinary believers how to share the gospel in natural and effective ways while being the person God made them to be.

Participants experience six 50-minute sessions:

- The Benefits of Becoming a Contagious Christian
- Being Yourself- and Impacting Others
- Deepening Your Relationships and Conversations
- Telling Your Story
- Communicating God's Message
- Helping Your Friends Cross the Line of Faith
- All-new vignettes, including dramas, interviews, and person-on-the-street segments

DVD 978-0-310-25788-2
Participant's Guide 978-0-310-25787-5
Leader's Guide 978-0-310-25786-8

Pick up a copy today at your favorite bookstore!

Share Your Thoughts

With the Author: Your comments will be forwarded to the author when you send them to *zauthor@zondervan.com*.

With Zondervan: Submit your review of this book by writing to *zreview@zondervan.com*.

Free Online Resources at
www.zondervan.com/hello

 Zondervan AuthorTracker: Be notified whenever your favorite authors publish new books, go on tour, or post an update about what's happening in their lives.

 Daily Bible Verses and Devotions: Enrich your life with daily Bible verses or devotions that help you start every morning focused on God.

 Free Email Publications: Sign up for newsletters on fiction, Christian living, church ministry, parenting, and more.

 Zondervan Bible Search: Find and compare Bible passages in a variety of translations at www.zondervanbiblesearch.com.

 Other Benefits: Register yourself to receive online benefits like coupons and special offers, or to participate in research.